MN

W9-APS-149

Pierre-Auguste Renoir

ABDO Publishing Company

Adam G. Klein

visit us at
www.abdopublishing.com

Printed in the United States.

Cover Photo: Corbis
Interior Photos: Art Resource pp. 5, 23, 25, 27; Bridgeman Art Library pp. 1, 4, 9, 11, 14, 17, 19,
    21, 29; Corbis pp. 8, 13, 15, 17, 26

Series Coordinator: Megan M. Gunderson
Editors: Heidi M. Dahmes, Megan M. Gunderson
Art Direction: Neil Klinepier

Library of Congress Cataloging-in-Publication Data

Klein, Adam G., 1976-
 Pierre-Auguste Renoir / Adam G. Klein
     p. cm. -- (Great artists)
 Includes index.
 ISBN-10 1-59679-736-3
 ISBN-13 978-1-59679-736-9
 1. Renoir, Auguste, 1841-1919--Juvenile literature. 2. Painters--France--Biography--Juvenile
literature. 3. Impressionism (Art)--France--Juvenile literature. I. Renoir, Auguste, 1841-1919. II.
Title III. Series: Klein, Adam G., 1976- . Great artists.

ND553.R45K54 2006
759.4--dc22
                                                                2005017894

Contents

Pierre-Auguste Renoir

Pierre-Auguste Renoir's paintings are some of the most recognizable works of art today. His images can be found on anything from umbrellas to calendars. But, this was not always the case. Renoir spent many years struggling to earn a living.

The world in the late 1800s was changing rapidly. Like many artists of his time, Renoir was caught between the old way of living and the new. There was a clash between old art and new art, as well. Some artists struggled to find their place in the art world. So, they created Impressionism.

Renoir was part of the Impressionist movement. He painted portraits, landscapes,

Renoir in 1885

and scenes from everyday life. Like many Impressionists, he often painted outdoors. This allowed him to capture moments as they happened. And, Renoir used brilliant colors and creative brushstrokes to produce beautiful works of art.

Before Renoir, artists used black to create shadows. Renoir used purple to create shadows in his sunny painting The Swing.

Timeline

1841 ~ On February 25, Pierre-Auguste Renoir was born in Limoges, France.

1860 to 1864 ~ Renoir was a registered copyist at the Louvre.

1862 ~ Renoir began studying at the École des Beaux-Arts; he painted *Return of the Boating Party*.

1864 ~ The Salon accepted *Esmeralda Dancing Before the Tramps*.

1866 ~ Renoir painted *At Mother Antony's*.

1868 ~ The Salon accepted *Lise with a Parasol*.

1872 ~ Art dealer Paul Durand-Ruel bought *Le Pont des Arts*.

1876 ~ Renoir painted *Dancing at the Moulin de la Galette*.

1878 ~ The Salon accepted *The Cup of Chocolate*.

1879 ~ *Madame Charpentier and Her Children* was a success at the Salon.

1900 ~ Renoir exhibited 11 works at the Paris Universal Exhibition.

1913 ~ Renoir took on sculpting with the help of his assistant, Richard Guino.

1919 ~ Renoir died on December 3.

Fun Facts

- From a young age, Pierre-Auguste Renoir liked to observe people. He loved watching people stroll by in the market in the Halles in Paris. He could study the same people while hidden behind the organ casing at St. Eustache on Sundays. Later, Renoir became known for painting people he observed in everyday settings.

- After working in the porcelain factory, Renoir earned extra money by painting window coverings. The speed of his work seemed unbelievable to his employer. But, Renoir's work was of such a high quality that he continued to be successful.

- Renoir decorated more than 20 cafés in Paris. At one café, Renoir got the job by proving he could work as fast as three men.

- Renoir often created paintings with similar themes. He completed several works that showed the Moulin de la Galette. In 1990, his painting *Au Moulin de la Galette* sold at auction for $78.1 million. It is one of the most expensive paintings ever sold.

Pierre-Auguste Renoir was born on February 25, 1841, in Limoges, France. He was one of seven children in his family. His father, Léonard Renoir, was a tailor. His mother, Marguerite Merlet, worked as a **seamstress**.

Around 1845, the Renoir family moved to Paris, France. They lived very close to the Louvre, a famous museum and art gallery. In Paris, Auguste went to a local church school.

The Renoirs attended the church of St. Eustache in the Halles district of Paris. There, Auguste sang in the choir. His teacher, Charles-François Gounod, discovered Auguste had a talent for singing. He suggested Auguste become an opera singer. But, Léonard and Marguerite had a different idea.

Charles-François Gounod later became famous for composing operas.

One of Renoir's favorite places in Paris was the market in the Halles.
This is artist Felix Benoist's vision of the market as seen from St. Eustache.

At that time, a person could make a fine living as a **porcelain** painter. As far as his parents were concerned, Auguste would do the same. So at age 13, Auguste was **apprenticed** to a porcelain factory. There, he would learn how to paint **ceramics**.

Porcelain

During his four-year **apprenticeship**, Auguste learned many skills. He painted everything from flowers and birds to country scenes and profiles of famous people.

Auguste soon became one of the most talented workers at the factory. But, he did not earn much money. So, a fellow worker shared paints and supplies with the struggling young artist.

By this time, Europe was in the middle of the **Industrial Revolution**. Inventions were changing the way people lived. However, not all of these changes were good for everyone. A machine was invented that could create prints on **porcelain** objects. So, Auguste's job was no longer necessary. He had to find a new career.

Auguste found small jobs to occupy his time. And, he continued improving his art. From 1860 to 1864, he was a registered copyist at the Louvre. This meant he was allowed to visit the museum to copy the work of other artists.

*Renoir's early work with porcelain influenced
his painting. Throughout his life, he painted
beautiful flowers, even in his portraits.*

Art School

By April 1862, Renoir had saved enough money to attend the École des Beaux-Arts in Paris. And, he had a painting teacher outside of school. Charles Gleyre encouraged the individual styles of all of his students.

Renoir made friends with Gleyre's other students, including Claude Monet, Alfred Sisley, and Jean-Frédéric Bazille. They all worked together out in the sun. During this time, Renoir painted *Return of the Boating Party*. This was the first of his many country-outing scenes.

One day while Renoir was out painting, artist Narcisse-Virgile Diaz de La Peña criticized his work. He told Renoir not to paint in such dark shades. Later, Renoir shocked other artists when he used blue to paint trees and purple for the earth! Diaz became a good friend to Renoir. He provided Renoir with supplies and advice when needed.

The Salon

The Salon was an important exhibition in France. It was named for the Salon d'Apollon in the Louvre, which is where each exhibition was held. The Salon became an annual event in the mid-1700s. And in the late 1700s, the event was opened to all French artists.

The Salon judges were a collection of teachers and elected officials. This jury would either accept a painting or reject it. The paintings that were well received at the Salon would be accepted by French society. This often helped an artist become successful.

The Salon jury had very strict guidelines for what it would accept. Renoir's painting Nymph and Faun *was one of many works rejected in 1863. That year, many artists participated in a separate event, the Salon des Refusés, or The Salon of the Refused.*

Vue perspective du Sallon de l'Academie Royale de Peinture et de Sculpture au Louvre, a Paris.

Gleyre's studio closed in 1864. That same year, Renoir had a painting accepted at the Salon for the first time. But, he destroyed *Esmeralda Dancing Before the Tramps* after the show.

The Early Years

By spring 1864, Renoir was spending a lot of time painting with his friends. They painted along the Seine River, by the Louvre, and in the forest of Fontainebleau near Paris.

Renoir almost always worked from models, including his friends. So, many people that he knew ended up in his paintings. *At Mother Antony's*, from 1866, features both Monet and Sisley.

Over the next few years, Renoir had some recognition at the Salon. In 1868, *Lise with a Parasol* was accepted. Still, Renoir lived with various artists to save money. Both he and Monet lived with Bazille for a while. And in 1869, Renoir moved in with the parents of his model Lise Tréhot.

Renoir painted **Frédéric Bazille at His Easel** *in 1867.*

The Barbizon painters believed in painting outdoors. Their work contributed partly to the Impressionist movement. Today, painters of the Barbizon school continue to paint in the forest of Fontainebleau.

Capturing Life

Renoir was known by his friends as relaxed, intelligent, and quiet. He and his friends spent many nights together at the Café Guerbois. There, they happily argued about life, politics, and art.

In 1869, Renoir and Monet spent time near the Seine. There, they completed the first Impressionist works. They painted summer scenes of boats, people, and especially water. Their paintings captured the variety of colors light created on water. This would become a common interest for the Impressionists.

In 1870, the **Franco-Prussian War** scattered the group of friends. Some artists fought in the war, while others fled the country. Renoir joined the French army. He was sent to Libourne, France, but never saw battle.

Artist's Corner

In 1874, journalist Louis Leroy came up with the term *Impressionism*. The label came from Claude Monet's painting *Impression: Sunrise*. Leroy originally meant it as an insult. But the name stuck, because it perfectly described what the artists were attempting to do. They wanted to show their impressions of moments in time.

At the time, most artists just sketched outdoor scenes. Then, they completed their paintings in a studio. But, Renoir and the other Impressionists completed paintings entirely outdoors. In this way, they could capture moments of daily life.

Many Impressionist paintings also emphasize the play of light on water. Renoir experimented with this theme. He and Monet painted several similar but distinct views of La Grenouillère, a resort on the Seine. They used small brushstrokes and bright colors. All of these elements were important to the Impressionist painters.

Renoir painted **La Grenouillère (left)** *in 1869. Monet's painting of the same scene* **(right)** *emphasizes the landscape more than the people.*

Impressionism

Renoir returned to Paris in mid-1871. He spent the next few years getting back in touch with his friends. During the war, Monet had met art dealer Paul Durand-Ruel.

Durand-Ruel became a huge supporter of Impressionism. In the following years, he helped Renoir and other struggling artists sell their work. Renoir sold him *Le Pont des Arts* in 1872.

The Impressionists held their first exhibition in 1874 at photographer Nadar's house. Nadar had met many of the Impressionists at the Café Guerbois. Renoir, Monet, Sisley, Camille Pissarro, and Paul Cézanne all participated in the show.

The Impressionist works were not popular at first. Some people disliked the way that the paintings seemed unfinished. They didn't take the artists seriously. And, some felt that the painters were troublemakers. They did not understand that the artists were trying to capture everyday moments.

Le Pont des Arts was influenced by photography, which was another popular new art form. Impressionist painters tried to capture moments in time, just as photographers could.

Acceptance

Despite the criticism, the Impressionist painters continued their work. Renoir finished *Dancing at the Moulin de la Galette* in 1876. It is often considered one of the most beautiful paintings ever created. It shows young Parisians spending time at an open-air dance hall. Renoir liked painting people. Even his landscapes usually include people.

Artists who showed their work at the Salon could not also exhibit with the Impressionists. Renoir decided not to enter the next Impressionist show. Instead, he submitted work to the Salon again. Renoir thought this would help him earn more **clients**.

The Salon accepted Renoir's 1878 painting *The Cup of Chocolate*. The next year, he found success with *Madame Charpentier and Her Children*. Madame Charpentier made sure the painting was displayed where everyone could see it. Renoir gained more customers from his success at the Salon.

Renoir painted Luncheon of the Boating Party (above) *just a few years after* Dancing at the Moulin de la Galette.

Moving On

Because of his newfound success, Renoir decided to travel. In March 1881, he took a vacation to Algeria to find inspiration. He also traveled to Italy, where he gained a new appreciation for classical paintings.

In 1882, Durand-Ruel showed 25 Renoir paintings at an Impressionist exhibition. But Renoir was trying to distance himself from the Impressionist group, which eventually broke apart.

Around this time, Renoir began to experiment with his work. He was looking for his own style. He felt there was room for improvement in his art.

Renoir did not like to be stuck in one style. So, he began to include classical elements in his work. This included a focus on simplicity. And, he used sharper lines to define his figures. Cézanne helped Renoir through these changes. Together, they found a new focus on classical traditions.

Renoir was always known for his use of color. But in the 1880s, he experimented with the use of black. He finished Girls Dressed in Black (left) *in 1881, and* The Umbrellas (right) *in 1883.*

Meanwhile, Renoir had fallen in love and married one of his models, Aline Charigot. She had supported him during his reinvention. Their first son, Pierre, was born in 1885. With enthusiasm, Renoir began painting scenes based on family life.

His Own Style

In 1894, Auguste and Aline's second son, Jean, was born. Their third son, Claude, was born in 1901. Renoir spent less time on his paintings during this period. He wanted to spend more time with his family. And, he doubted the value of his own work.

Also in 1894, Renoir had his first attack of **rheumatism**. As a result, Renoir sometimes walked with a cane. And, he began spending more time in southern France. There, the warmer weather eased the pain in his joints.

By 1895, Renoir's paintings show his attempt to combine classical elements with Impressionism. He used softer colors again, but he concentrated on using fewer colors at a time. Sunlight still inspired Renoir. So, he used colors that reflected that interest.

In 1899, Durand-Ruel exhibited another 41 Renoir works. Renoir's art was selling for high prices. Still, he struggled with money because of his expensive lifestyle.

In the mid-1890s, a client requested Renoir's Young Girls at the Piano. Doubting its value, Renoir created five new paintings on the subject. The client was shocked that he was given so many to choose from!

Honors

In 1900, Renoir exhibited 11 works at the Paris Universal Exhibition. The same year, Renoir was made a chevalier of the Legion of Honor. This is like being knighted, which means Renoir was honored for his contributions to France.

Renoir's art still reflected the beauty and love for life that he had in his youth. The number of people who appreciated his work grew. Early in his career, the Salon had rejected him. But by 1900, Renoir's artwork was selling for more than 20,000 francs per painting. Today, this would be more than $80,000.

Late in life, Renoir often used a wheelchair.

Renoir moved to Les Collettes in 1908. There, he had two indoor studios as well as an outdoor studio.

By 1910, Renoir's health was worsening. His hands became more deformed every day from the **rheumatism**. Soon, he could no longer hold a paintbrush properly. So, Renoir pinched his brushes between his fingers or strapped them to his hands. This worked well for him, and he continued to create beautiful paintings and to gain admirers.

Sculpting

Around 1913, Renoir worked in sculpture. The sculptures were modeled after his drawings and paintings. But by this time, Renoir's **rheumatism** was severe. So, he gave directions to his assistant, Richard Guino. Guino changed each sculpture until it pleased Renoir. This way, the works still reflect Renoir's style.

World War I began in 1914. Renoir's older sons, Pierre and Jean, went off to fight. They were both wounded in early 1915. Both sons recovered from their injuries, but Aline died soon after visiting Jean.

Despite his illness, Renoir continued to paint. On December 3, 1919, he worked on a painting of flowers. He died later that day from **pneumonia**.

The old masters and other talented artists inspired Renoir. He in turn inspired generations of artists after him. Renoir helped people find beauty in everyday things.

Since 1907, Madame Charpentier and Her Children (above) *has been part of the collection of the Metropolitan Museum of Art in New York City, New York. Renoir's other portrait of Madame Charpentier was hung in the Louvre in 1919. This proved to Renoir that he and the other Impressionists were finally appreciated.*

Glossary

apprentice - a person who learns a trade or a craft from a skilled worker.

ceramic - of or relating to a nonmetallic product, such as pottery or porcelain.

client - a person who hires or uses the services of a professional of some type.

Franco-Prussian War - from 1870 to 1871. A war fought between France and Prussia, a former kingdom now in Germany. Prussia won the war and created the German Empire.

Industrial Revolution - the period in the 1800s when new machinery and technology changed the world economy.

pneumonia - a disease that affects the lungs and may cause fever, coughing, or difficulty breathing.

porcelain - a fine, hard, white ceramic material.

rheumatism - a medical condition causing swelling and pain in the joints and the muscles. Rheumatism is similar to arthritis.

seamstress - a woman who sews clothes.

World War I - from 1914 to 1918, fought in Europe. Great Britain, France, Russia, the United States, and their allies were on one side. Germany, Austria-Hungary, and their allies were on the other side.

Saying It

Alfred Sisley - awl-frehd see-slay
Charles-François Gounod - shawrl-frahn-swaw goo-noh
École des Beaux-Arts - ay-KAWL day boh-ZAHR
Fontainebleau - fawn-tehn-BLOH
Limoges - lee-MOHZH
Louvre - LOO-vruh
Paul Cézanne - pawl say-zawn
Seine - SEHN

Web Sites

To learn more about Pierre-Auguste Renoir, visit ABDO Publishing Company on the World Wide Web at **www.abdopublishing.com**. Web sites about Renoir are featured on our Book Links page. These links are routinely monitored and updated to provide the most current information available.

Index